Grades K-2

Guided MATH Workstations

Authors

Donna Boucher

Laney Sammons, M.L.S.

SHELL EDUCATION

For information on how this resource meets national and other state standards, see pages 13–14. You may also review this information by visiting our website at www.teachercreatedmaterials.com/administrators/correlations/ and following the on-screen directions.

Publishing Credits

Corinne Burton, M.A.Ed., *President*; Conni Medina, M.A.Ed., *Managing Editor*; Diana Kenney M.A.Ed., NBCT, *Content Director*; Veronique Bos, *Creative Director*; Robin Erickson, *Art Director*; Kristy Stark, M.A.Ed., *Editor*; Fabiola Sepulveda, *Graphic Designer*; Kyleena Harper, *Assistant Editor*

Image Credits

All images from iStock and Shutterstock.

Standards

Shell Education

A division of Teacher Created Materials
5301 Oceanus Drive
Huntington Beach, CA 92649-1030

http://www.tcmpub.com/shell-education

ISBN 978-1-4258-1728-2
©2018 Shell Educational Publishing, Inc.
Printed in USA. WOR004

Table of Contents

Introduction

GUIDE Workstation Tasks

Games for **Mathematicians**

Using What **We Know**

Table of Contents *(cont.)*

Independent Math Work

Developing Fluency

Expressing Mathematical Ideas

Appendices

The Guided Math Framework

Guided Math (Sammons 2010, 2014) is an instructional framework that helps teachers provide quality mathematics instruction for their students. Teachers address their students' varied learning needs within a carefully planned numeracy-rich environment where students are challenged to not just *do* math but instead *become* mathematicians. Implemented together, Guided Math's seven components are designed to help students as they develop a deep conceptual understanding of math, acquire computational fluency, and become skilled in thinking and acting mathematically.

Figure I.1 Instructional Components of Guided Math

Classroom Environment of Numeracy (Daily)
Students are immersed in a classroom environment that contains evidence of real-life math tasks, data analysis, math word walls, measuring tools, mathematical communication, class-created math anchor charts, graphic organizers, calendars, and authentic problem-solving challenges.
Math Warm-Ups (Daily)
This daily appetizer prepares students for "Your Choice" entrees with Math Stretches, calendar activities, problems of the day, reviews of skills to be maintained, and previews of skills to come.
Whole-Class Instruction (Your Choice)
Students are instructed as a whole group to activate prior knowledge, to model and think aloud, to read math-related literature aloud, to review and assess, or for Math Huddles.
Small-Group Instruction (Your Choice)
Students are instructed in small groups based on student needs to introduce new concepts, practice new skills, work with manipulatives, provide intensive and targeted instruction to struggling learners, provide additional challenge, introduce Math Workshop activities, and conduct informal assessments.
Math Workshop (Your Choice)
Students work independently, either individually, in pairs, or in groups, on tasks that may include extensions of other activities, mastered skills, investigations, math games, math journals, or interdisciplinary work, while teachers conduct small-group lessons and conferences.
Conferences (Daily)
Teachers confer with students to assess understanding, provide opportunities for math communication, determine instructional needs, and deliver brief teaching points.
Assessment (Daily)
Students are assessed through observation, on final work products, and during mathematical conversations. Assessment *for* learning and *of* learning are key to informing instruction.

(Sammons 2010)

What Is Math Workshop?

Math Workshop is a key ingredient of success in a Guided Math classroom (Sammons 2010, 2013). As one of the most versatile components of the framework, it accommodates a vast array of learning tasks. Not only does it provide opportunities for students to learn how to work independently on worthwhile mathematical endeavors, it also allows teachers to work with small groups or to confer with individual students.

During Math Workshop, students work independently—individually, in pairs, or in groups—and participate in Math Workstation tasks that have been designed to provide ongoing practice of previously mastered concepts and skills, to promote computational fluency, and to encourage mathematical curiosity and inquiry. In the first weeks of school, students learn and repeatedly practice the routines and procedures that make Math Workshop function smoothly. As students assume greater independence for their learning during Math Workshop, teachers may then expand their teaching roles.

Figure I.2 The Roles of Teachers and Students during Math Workshop

Teachers	Students
• Teach small-group lessons • Conduct math conferences • Informally assess learning through observations • Facilitate mathematical learning and curiosity through questioning	• Assume responsibility for their learning and behavior • Function as fledgling mathematicians • Communicate mathematically with peers • Review and practice previously mastered concepts and skills • Improve computational fluency • Increase ability to work cooperatively with peers

What Are Math Workstations?

Workstations are collections of tasks stored together and worked on independently of the teacher by students in specified workspaces. Students often work in pairs or small groups but may work alone. Each station contains a variety of carefully selected math tasks to support mathematical learning. Some of the tasks may be mandatory, while others may be optional. Essential for an effective Math Workshop is the inclusion of high-quality, appropriate tasks in the workstations. By grappling with these tasks independently, students gain greater mathematical proficiency and confidence in their mathematical abilities. Here, students "practice problem solving while reasoning, representing, communicating, and making connections among mathematical topics as the teacher observes and interacts with individuals at work or meets with a small group for differentiated math instruction" (Diller 2011, 7).

Math Centers versus Math Workstations

For many years, classrooms contained Math Centers where learners worked independently. Math Centers were considerably different from today's Math Workstations. Even the label *Math Workstation* clearly sends the message that students are expected to work as mathematicians. Workstation tasks are not included for fun alone but to further students' understanding of math, improve their computational fluency, and increase their mathematical competency. The chart below highlights the differences between Math Centers and Math Workstations.

Figure I.3 Math Centers versus Math Workstations

Math Centers	Math Workstations
• Games and activities are introduced to students when distributed at centers and are rarely used for instructional purposes.	• Tasks are derived from materials previously used during instruction, so students are already familiar with them.
• Centers are often thematic and change weekly.	• Tasks are changed for instructional purposes, not because it is the end of the week.
• Centers are often made available to students after they complete their regular work.	• Tasks provide ongoing practice to help students retain and deepen their understanding and are an important part of students' mathematical instruction.
• All students work on the same centers, and activities are seldom differentiated.	• Tasks are differentiated to meet the identified learning needs of students.

The GUIDE Model

The GUIDE model provides a simple and efficient organizational system for Math Workshop. With this model there are five Math Workstations, each with a menu of tasks from which students may work. The workstation tasks may be required, optional, or a combination of the two. You as the teacher decide which best meets the needs of your students. Instead of rotating from station to station, students work on only one station per day. By the end of a week, however, students will have worked at all five GUIDE stations.

The GUIDE acronym stands for the following:

Games for Mathematicians: Math games used to maintain previously mastered mathematical concepts and skills and promote computational proficiency

Using What We Know: Problem solving or challenge activities to draw upon mathematical understanding and skills

Independent Math Work: Materials used to teach previously mastered content incorporated into workstation tasks (paper-and-pencil tasks may be included)

Developing Fluency: Tasks that help students develop number sense and mental math skills

Expressing Mathematical Ideas: Tasks with opportunities to solidify mathematical vocabulary and encourage communication (math journals or math vocabulary notebooks may be included)

Students may be given the choice of where they will work each day, or the teacher may make team assignments. If you allow your students to choose their stations, provide a weekly checklist to track completed stations. Using the checklist, they will clearly see which stations they still need to complete by the end of the week.

This model offers maximum flexibility to teachers. Not only can the composition of small-group lessons be changed at a moment's notice to respond to newly identified student needs, but the length of the lessons may also vary from group to group. Teachers also appreciate another aspect of the flexibility this model offers. If the Math Workshop schedule is interrupted for some reason (e.g., testing day, holiday, whole-group lesson), the rotation schedule simply continues the next day as Math Workshop resumes. So, if a student does *G* on Monday, *U* on Tuesday, and then there is no workshop on Wednesday, he or she would do *I* on Thursday. As a result, students might not do all five workstations in one week, but they would still get to do them all after five Math Workshop days.

Differentiating Math Workstation Tasks

It is important that workstation tasks are differentiated to meet the unique needs of learners. Task Menus should clearly indicate which tasks have these options, and directions for these tasks should explain each of the options. Students need to know not only what the options are, but also which of them they should complete. Rather than labeling the options by ability level, various options for differentiation may be indicated by color, shape, or other symbol. For example, if there are three options, one might be coded with a circle, one with a triangle, and one with a square. Let students know which options they will complete by assigning them to the shape that best meets their learning needs.

While much focus has been placed on differentiation for struggling students, differentiation for those who may need extra challenge is equally important. There are several ways to provide differentiation. Tasks may be differentiated by:

- **Providing completely different tasks**—In some instances, students at one workstation will work on completely different tasks to address identified needs.

- **Providing variations of the same task**—This is the most efficient way to differentiate Math Workstation tasks because students work on the same task with some variations, so it can be introduced to everyone at the same time rather than having to introduce different tasks for different students. The task might be differentiated by changing the numbers, operations involved, or other aspects of the task to make it appropriate for all learners. Students who struggle with reading may require a recording of the task directions or other written materials. Some students may need to have manipulatives available. Others may benefit from having vocabulary cards with visual representations as references. Consider students' needs and offer support, if necessary, but use your professional judgment to avoid providing ongoing supports that become crutches rather than scaffolds for learning. Each task provided in this resource offers suggestions for differentiation to address individual students' needs.

- **Providing multiple ways for students to show their learning**—Students who struggle may benefit from the use of manipulatives to demonstrate their mathematical understanding. Students who need a challenge may create graphic organizers to display their work or graphs to represent data.

How to Use This Book

The tasks in this book have been designed for use with the GUIDE Workshop Model, but they may be incorporated into any workshop model you choose. It is important to model and practice these workstation tasks and the sentence stems on the *Talking Points* cards with students before expecting students to complete them independently.

Workstation Organization

An **overview** of the lesson, materials, objective, procedure, and differentiation is provided for the teacher on the first page of each GUIDE workstation task.

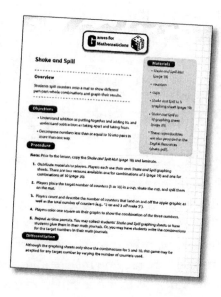

A **Student Task card** with directions and a materials list is provided for easy implementation and organization. Students may use the materials list as they put away their math workstation task so that all materials are included.

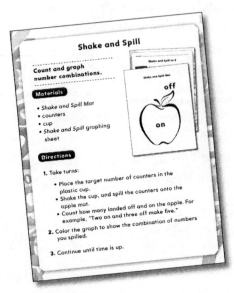

A **Talking Points card** with math vocabulary words and sentence stems is provided to encourage mathematical discourse. Consider copying it on brightly colored paper to draw students' attention. Laminate and store it with the student task card and other resources for each workstation task.

Additional **resources** for each task (e.g., spinners, cards, activity sheets) are included.

Digital resources to support the workstation tasks in this book are available online. A complete list of available documents is provided on pages 143. To access the digital resources, go to this website: **http://www.tcmpub.com/download-files**. Enter this code: 89478772. Follow the on-screen directions.

Introduction to Standards Correlations

Shell Educational Publishing is committed to producing educational materials that are research- and standards-based. In this effort, we have correlated all of our products to the academic standards of all 50 states, the District of Columbia, the Department of Defense Dependents Schools, and all Canadian provinces.

How to Find Standards Correlations

To print a customized correlation report of this product for your state, visit our website at **http://www.tcmpub.com/shell-education**. If you require assistance in printing correlation reports, please contact our Customer Service Department at 1-877-777-3450.

Purpose and Intent of Standards

The Every Student Succeeds Act (ESSA) mandates that all states adopt challenging academic standards that help students meet the goal of college and career readiness. While many states already adopted academic standards prior to ESSA, the act continues to hold states accountable for detailed and comprehensive standards.

Standards are designed to focus instruction and guide adoption of curricula. Standards are statements that describe the criteria necessary for students to meet specific academic goals. They define the knowledge, skills, and content students should acquire at each level. Standards are also used to develop standardized tests to evaluate students' academic progress.

Teachers are required to demonstrate how their lessons meet state standards. State standards are used in the development of all of our products, so educators can be assured they meet the academic requirements of each state.

The workstation tasks in this book are aligned to today's national and state-specific college-and-career readiness standards. The chart on pages 13–14 shows the correlation of those standards to the workstation tasks.

Standards Correlations

Workstation Task	College-and-Career Readiness Standard(s)
Shake and Spill (page 15)	Understand addition as putting together and adding to and subtraction as taking apart and taking from. Decompose numbers less than or equal to 10 into pairs in more than one way.
Squeeze Play (page 21)	Solve addition equations Understand the meaning of the equal sign.
Race to the Bottom (page 26)	Use place value understanding and properties of operations to add and subtract (mentally find 10 more or 10 less).
Crazy Clock Keep-Away (page 31)	Tell and write time to the nearest five minutes using analog and digital clocks.
Exploring Manipulatives (page 40)	Make sense of problems and persevere in solving them.
Polygon Pictures (page 43)	Reason with shapes and their attributes.
You Write the Story (page 47)	Represent and solve problems involving addition and subtraction.
What Is the Question? (page 53)	Solve simple join, separate, and compare problems using information presented in graphs and tables.
Representing Numbers (page 60)	Represent numbers to 120 in standard form, pictorial form, and expanded form.
Missing Number Puzzles (page 68)	Use place value understanding and properties of addition to add and subtract.

Piggy Bank Problems (page 74)	Find the value of a collection of coins.
Numberless Word Problems (page 82)	Use addition and subtraction to solve word problems involving situations of joining, separating, part-part-whole, and comparing, with unknowns in any position.
Make 5, Capture 4 (page 91)	Fluently add and subtract within 10.
Make 10, Capture 4 (page 97)	For any number 1–9, find the number that makes 10 when added to the given number.
Addition Move One (page 103)	Add and subtract within 20 using mental strategies.
Sum or Difference (page 108)	Add and subtract within 100.
Par for the Course (page 120)	Add and subtract to build automaticity with math facts.
Math Vocabulary Book (page 125)	Communicate precisely, using clear definitions when discussing and reasoning about mathematics.
Survey Says… (page 134)	Organize, represent, and interpret data with up to three categories.
All About… (page 139)	Use precise mathematical language, numbers, and/or drawings to represent a mathematical concept.

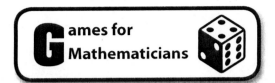

Games for **Mathematicians**

Shake and Spill

- -

Overview

Students spill counters onto a mat to show different part-part-whole combinations and graph their results.

- -

Objectives

- Understand addition as putting together and adding to and subtraction as taking apart and taking from.

- Decompose numbers less than or equal to 10 into pairs in more than one way.

Procedure

Note: Prior to the lesson, copy the *Shake and Spill Mat* (page 18) and laminate.

1. Distribute materials to players. Players each use their own *Shake and Spill* graphing sheets. There are two versions available: one for combinations of 5 (page 19) and one for combinations of 10 (page 20).

2. Players place the target number of counters (5 or 10) in a cup, shake the cup, and spill them on the mat.

3. Players count and describe the number of counters that land *on* and *off* the apple graphic as well as the total number of counters (e.g., "2 *on* and 3 *off* make 5").

4. Players color one square on their graphs to show the combination of the three numbers.

5. Repeat as time permits. You may collect students' *Shake and Spill* graphing sheets or have students glue them in their math journals. Or, you may have students write the combinations for the target numbers in their math journals.

Differentiation

Although the graphing sheets only show the combinations for 5 and 10, this game may be adapted for any target number by varying the number of counters used.

Materials

- *Shake and Spill Mat* (page 18)

- counters

- cups

- *Shake and Spill* to 5 graphing sheet (page 19)

- *Shake and Spill* to 10 graphing sheet (page 20)

* The *Talking Points* card and these reproducibles are also provided in the Digital Resources (shake.pdf).

Shake and Spill

Count and graph number combinations.

Materials

- *Shake and Spill Mat*
- counters
- cup
- *Shake and Spill* graphing sheet

Directions

1. Take turns:

- Place the target number of counters in the plastic cup.
- Shake the cup, and spill the counters onto the apple mat.
- Count and tell how many landed off and on the apple. For example, "Two on and three off make five."

2. Color the graph to show the combination of numbers you spilled.

3. Continue until time is up.

Talking Points

Vocabulary
• addition
• combination
$$3 + 5 = 8$$ addends sum

Talk like a mathematician:

_____ *on* the apple and _____ *off* the apple make _____.

_____ and _____ make _____.

My addends are _____ and _____.

My sum is _____.

When I look at the graph, I notice _____.

✂ -

Talking Points

Vocabulary
• addition
• combination
$$3 + 5 = 8$$ addends sum

Talk like a mathematician:

_____ *on* the apple and _____ *off* the apple make _____.

_____ and _____ make _____.

My addends are _____ and _____.

My sum is _____.

When I look at the graph, I notice _____.

Shake and Spill Mat

off

on

51728—Guided Math Workstations

© Shell Education

Shake and Spill to 5

Directions: Color a square to show each combination of 5 that you shake and spill.

10						
9						
8						
7						
6						
5						
4						
3						
2						
1						
	0 on 5 off	1 on 4 off	2 on 3 off	3 on 2 off	4 on 1 off	5 on 0 off
	0 +5	1 +4	2 +3	3 +2	4 +1	5 +0

Shake and Spill to 10

Directions: Color a square to show each combination of 10 that you *shake* and *spill*.

10											
9											
8											
7											
6											
5											
4											
3											
2											
1											
	0 on 10 off	1 on 9 off	2 on 8 off	3 on 7 off	4 on 6 off	5 on 5 off	6 on 4 off	7 on 3 off	8 on 2 off	9 on 1 off	10 on 0 off
	0 + 10	**1 + 9**	**2 + 8**	**3 + 7**	**4 + 6**	**5 + 5**	**6 + 4**	**7 + 3**	**8 + 2**	**9 + 1**	**10 + 0**

51728—Guided Math Workstations

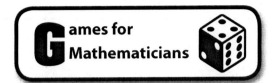

Squeeze Play

Overview

Students use digits on number cards to create equations.

Objectives

- Solve addition equations.
- Understand the meaning of the equal sign.

Procedure

Note: Prior to the lesson, make four copies of the *Squeeze Play Number Cards* (page 24) on cardstock, cut, and laminate.

1. Distribute copies of the *Squeeze Play* recording sheet (page 25) and other materials to each student.

2. Players place number cards facedown in the center of the playing area.

3. Players take turns turning over a number card and writing the number in one of the empty spaces on their recording sheet to create true equations.

4. Players should discuss their strategies for placing numbers and should justify each equation as completed.

5. When a player cannot place a number in an empty space, his or her turn is over.

6. Players may share their learning with the class by recording equations on index cards that can be displayed on a *Squeeze Play* wall or bulletin board. They could also add an entry to a *Squeeze Play* book that can be kept at the station.

7. You may choose to have students turn in their completed recording sheets or glue them in their math journals.

Differentiation

- Provide counters and ten frames or linking cubes for **below-level learners** for concrete support.

- Vary the number of cards used based on students need. Some students might only use cards 0–5, while other students use numbers up to 10. Challenge **above-level learners** with larger numbers.

Materials

- *Squeeze Play Number Cards* (page 24)

- *Squeeze Play* recording sheet (page 25)

- counters and ten frames or linking cubes (optional)

* The *Talking Points* card and these reproducibles are also provided in the Digital Resources (squeeze.pdf).

Squeeze Play

Place numbers in the spaces to create equations.

Materials

- *Squeeze Play Number Cards*
- *Squeeze Play* recording sheet
- counters and ten frames or linking cubes (optional)

Directions

1. Choose which player will go first.

2. Take turns:

- Turn over a number card.
- Write the number in an empty space on your *Squeeze Play* recording sheet.
- If you cannot fill in a space with the number you turned over, you lose your turn.

3. When you complete an equation, justify why it is true.

4. Complete all or the most equations first to win!

Talking Points

Vocabulary

- equal sign (=)
- plus (+)
- equation
- justify

$$2 + 3 = 5$$

addends sum

Talk like a mathematician:

_____ is equal to _____ because _____.

The sum of _____ and _____ is _____.

Another way to make _____ is _____.

My equation is true because _____.

The equal sign means _____.

Talking Points

Vocabulary

- equal sign (=)
- plus (+)
- equation
- justify

$$2 + 3 = 5$$

addends sum

Talk like a mathematician:

_____ is equal to _____ because _____.

The sum of _____ and _____ is _____.

Another way to make _____ is _____.

My equation is true because _____.

The equal sign means _____.

Squeeze Play Number Cards

0	1	2
3	4	5
6	7	8
9	10	

51728—Guided Math Workstations

Squeeze Play

☐ = ☐ + ☐

☐ = ☐ + ☐

☐ + ☐ = ☐

☐ = ☐ + ☐ + ☐

☐ + ☐ = ☐ + ☐

☐ + ☐ = ☐ + ☐

☐ + ☐ = ☐ + ☐

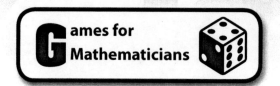

Race to the Bottom

Overview

Players attempt to reach the bottom row of the *120 Chart* by finding patterns in the chart (e.g., 10 more, 10 less, 1 more, 1 less).

Materials

- *120 Chart* (page 29)
- paper clip and pencil
- game markers
- *Race to the Bottom Spinner* (page 30)
- base-ten blocks (optional)

* The *Talking Points* card and these reproducibles are also provided in the Digital Resources (race.pdf).

Objective

Use place value understanding and properties of operations to add and subtract (mentally find 10 more or 10 less).

Procedure

1. Distribute copies of the *120 Chart* (page 29) and other materials to students.

2. Players place game markers on any space in the top row.

3. Taking turns, each player spins the spinner and moves his or her playing piece on the chart. For example, if a player is on 24 and spins *10 more*, the player may move 10 spaces on the chart by moving his or her playing piece down one row.

4. The first player to reach the bottom row wins.

5. Players may record their moves in their math journals using the sentence stems from the *Talking Points* card (e.g., *Ten more than 24 is 34.*).

Differentiation

- Provide base-ten blocks for **below-level learners** who need concrete support. This also allows students to practice regrouping. For example, if a student is on 20 and spins 1 less, he or she would need to trade a ten for 10 ones to subtract one.

- Use charts with larger numbers (e.g., 200–320 or 300–420) for **above-level learners** who are ready to work with a wider range of numbers.

Race to the Bottom

Be the first to reach the bottom row of the _120 Chart_!

120 Chart

1	2	3	4	5	6	7	8	9	10
11	12	13	14	15	16	17	18	19	20
21	22	23	24	25	26	27	28	29	30
31	32	33	34	35	36	37	38	39	40
41	42	43	44	45	46	47	48	49	50
51	52	53	54	55	56	57	58	59	60
61	62	63	64	65	66	67	68	69	70
71	72	73	74	75	76	77	78	79	80
81	82	83	84	85	86			89	90
91	92	93	94	9				0	
101	102	103	104						
111	112	113	114						

Spinner: 1 less / 1 more / 10 more / 10 less

Materials

- _120 Chart_
- paper clip and pencil
- game markers
- _Race to the Bottom Spinner_
- base-ten blocks (optional)

Directions

1. Place your game marker on any space in the first row.

2. Take turns:

- Spin the spinner.
- If you spin _10 less_ when you are on the first row, spin again.
- Move your playing piece.
- Explain your move. For example, "Ten more than 24 is 34."

3. Reach the bottom row first to win!

Talking Points

Vocabulary	Talk like a mathematician:
• column	Ten more than _____ is _____.
• row	Ten less than _____ is _____.
• pattern	One more than _____ is _____.
• one more →	One less than _____ is _____.
• one less ←	A pattern I see is _____.
• ten more ↓	
• ten less ↑	

✂ -

Talking Points

Vocabulary	Talk like a mathematician:
• column	Ten more than _____ is _____.
• row	Ten less than _____ is _____.
• pattern	One more than _____ is _____.
• one more →	One less than _____ is _____.
• one less ←	A pattern I see is _____.
• ten more ↓	
• ten less ↑	

120 Chart

1	2	3	4	5	6	7	8	9	10
11	12	13	14	15	16	17	18	19	20
21	22	23	24	25	26	27	28	29	30
31	32	33	34	35	36	37	38	39	40
41	42	43	44	45	46	47	48	49	50
51	52	53	54	55	56	57	58	59	60
61	62	63	64	65	66	67	68	69	70
71	72	73	74	75	76	77	78	79	80
81	82	83	84	85	86	87	88	89	90
91	92	93	94	95	96	97	98	99	100
101	102	103	104	105	106	107	108	109	110
111	112	113	114	115	116	117	118	119	120

Race to the Bottom Spinner

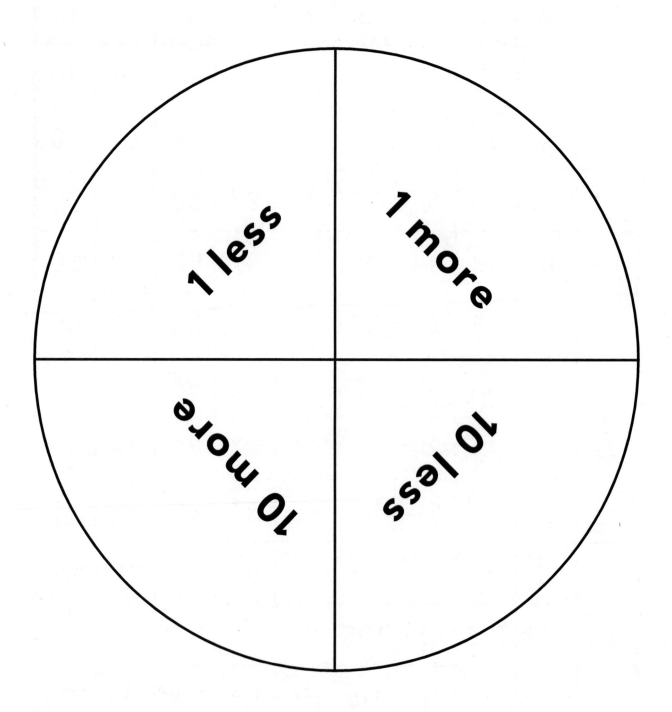

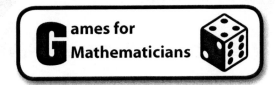

Crazy Clock Keep-Away

Overview

Students tell time using digital and analog clocks to collect matching cards in this twist on an Old Maid game.

Materials

- *Crazy Clock Keep-Away Cards* (pages 34–38)

- *Crazy Clock* recording sheet (page 39)

- student clocks (optional)

* The *Talking Points* card and these reproducibles are also provided in the Digital Resources (crazyclock.pdf).

Objective

Tell and write time to the nearest five minutes using analog and digital clocks.

Procedure

1. Copy the *Crazy Clock Keep-Away Cards* (pages 34–38) on cardstock, laminate, and cut apart.

2. Players shuffle the cards and distribute them evenly among themselves. Players do not need to have an equal number of cards.

3. Players look at their hands and immediately lay down any matching pairs of cards. Matching cards show a digital clock and an analog clock that reflect the same time.

4. The first player offers his or her hand facedown to the player on his or her left, who takes one card. If the card selected completes a match, the player sets aside the matching cards. Then, the player offers his or her hand facedown to the player on his or her left.

6. Play continues until only the crazy clock card is left. The player holding the crazy clock card loses the game.

7. At the end of the game, students record a maximum of nine of their cards on the *Crazy Clock* recording sheet (page 39). You may collect students' recording sheets or have students glue them in math journals.

Differentiation

- Provide student clocks to **below-level-learners** who need a more concrete activity. Also consider varying the cards used for the game. For example, students may use only the cards showing time on the hour or half-hour until they gain mastery at that level.

- Challenge **above-level learners** to choose pairs of cards and find the elapsed time between the times shown on the two cards.

Crazy Clock Keep-Away

Read times on digital and analog clocks to collect matching cards. Avoid the crazy clock!

Materials

- *Crazy Clock Keep-Away Cards*
- *Crazy Clock* recording sheet
- student clocks (optional)

Directions

1. Shuffle the cards. Give cards to each player until all cards are gone. It's okay if players don't get an equal number of cards.

2. Lay down any matching pairs of cards from your hand faceup. Matching cards will show a digital clock and an analog clock with the same time.

3. Player 1 offers cards, facedown, to the player on the left. That player takes one card. If the card completes a match, the second player lays down the pair. Player 2 then offers cards, facedown, to the player on the left.

4. Keep playing until only the Crazy Clock is left. The player with the Crazy Clock card loses the game.

5. Use the *Crazy Clock* recording sheet to show the times on nine cards.

Talking Points

Vocabulary	**Talk like a mathematician:**
• analog clock • digital clock • minute hand • hour hand • noon • midnight • a.m. • p.m.	I know my analog clock shows _____ because _____. (time) I can find the minutes on the clock by _____. I can find the hour on the clock by _____. An activity I do at _____ (a.m. or p.m.) is _____. (time)

✂ ┄┄

Talking Points

Vocabulary	**Talk like a mathematician:**
• analog clock • digital clock • minute hand • hour hand • noon • midnight • a.m. • p.m.	I know my analog clock shows _____ because _____. (time) I can find the minutes on the clock by _____. I can find the hour on the clock by _____. An activity I do at _____ (a.m. or p.m.) is _____. (time)

Crazy Clock Keep-Away Cards

1:00	(clock: 12:00)	1:40
(clock: 2:40)	2:30	(clock: 1:30)
2:50	(clock: 9:10)	3:00
(clock: 12:15)	3:20	(clock: 2:20)

Crazy Clock Keep-Away Cards *(cont.)*

Crazy Clock Keep-Away Cards *(cont.)*

51728—Guided Math Workstations

© *Shell Education*

Crazy Clock Keep-Away Cards *(cont.)*

Crazy Clock Keep-Away Cards *(cont.)*

Crazy Clock

Directions: Draw hands on the clocks to match the clocks shown on your cards. Write the time shown on the clock.

_____

_____

_____

_____

_____

_____

_____

_____

_____

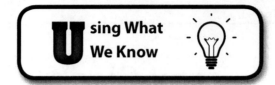

Using What We Know

Exploring Manipulatives

- -

Overview

Students engage in unstructured exploration of manipulatives in preparation for organized use during workstation tasks.

- -

Objective

Make sense of the problems and persevere in solving them.

Procedure

1. Place manipulatives in a workstation. Allow students time to explore with them prior to using the manipulative for more formal math activities.

2. Provide drawing or graph paper for students who choose to create drawings of their manipulatives or record their thinking.

3. Consider having students use digital devices to take pictures of their explorations or record one another explaining their observations about the manipulatives.

Differentiation

Due to the nature of this activity, it is accessible to students of all ability levels, and students will naturally differentiate their explorations.

Exploring Manipulatives

Explore math manipulatives, and describe your observations.

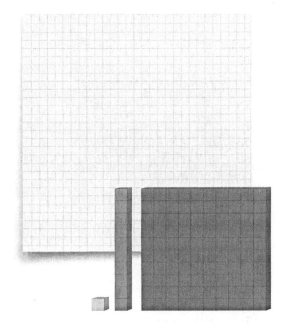

Materials

- math manipulatives
- digital device, drawing paper, or graph paper

Directions

1. Take time to freely explore a math manipulative.

2. Think about how it might be a useful tool for mathematicians.

3. Make observations about the manipulative using words and pictures.

Talking Points

Vocabulary	Talk like a mathematician:
• manipulative • attribute • observe • observations • sort	I noticed that _____. I wonder _____. This manipulative is a useful tool for mathematicians because _____. This manipulative reminds me of _____. I can sort my manipulatives by _____.

✂ -

Talking Points

Vocabulary	Talk like a mathematician:
• manipulative • attribute • observe • observations • sort	I noticed that _____. I wonder _____. This manipulative is a useful tool for mathematicians because _____. This manipulative reminds me of _____. I can sort my manipulatives by _____.

Using What We Know

Polygon Pictures

- -

Overview

Students use pattern blocks to create a picture or pattern, and describe the attributes of the shapes they used.

- -

Objective

Reason with shapes and their attributes.

Procedure

Note: Allow time for students to freely explore the pattern blocks prior to placing this task in a workstation. Explain to students that each piece in the pattern block set is a polygon because it is a closed shape with straight sides and that each piece also has a more specific name. Discuss the names and attributes of each pattern block piece.

1. Distribute copies of the *My Polygon Picture* recording sheet (page 46) and other materials to students.

3. Students use pattern blocks to create pictures or patterns.

4. Students trace their pictures on paper or take photographs of them.

5. Students write the number of each type of block they used and write number sentences to show the total number of blocks.

6. Students write three sentences describing the attributes of the polygons they used.

7. Students may draw their pictures in math journals or on recording sheets. Or, students may take photographs of their pictures using digital devices.

Differentiation

- Instruct **below-level learners** on the number of blocks they may use to limit the numbers they work with (e.g., numbers to 10).

- Have **above-level learners** try to recreate pictures using different pieces (e.g., a hexagon can be made with two trapezoids).

Materials

- *My Polygon Picture* recording sheet (page 46)

- pattern blocks

- digital device (optional)

* The *Talking Points* card and these reproducibles are also provided in the Digital Resources (polygon.pdf).

Polygon Pictures

Create a picture or pattern with pattern blocks. Tell about the number and type of blocks you used.

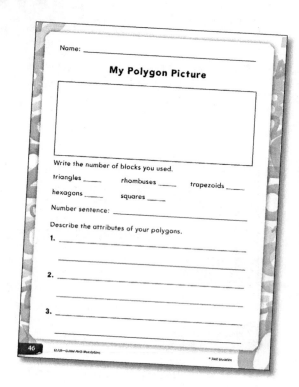

Materials

- *My Polygon Picture* recording sheet
- pattern blocks
- digital device (optional)

Directions

1. Use the pattern blocks to make a picture or pattern.

2. Trace your picture on paper and color it. Or, take a photo of it.

3. Count and write the number of blocks you used.

4. Write a number sentence to show how many blocks you used.

5. Write three sentences to tell about the attributes of your polygons.

Talking Points

Vocabulary

- polygon
- attribute
- hexagon
- rhombus
- square
- triangle
- trapezoid

Talk like a mathematician:

The attributes of a _____ are _____.
(shape)

A _____ is a polygon because _____.
(shape)

One way a _____ and a _____ are
(shape)   (shape)
the same is _____.

Talking Points

Vocabulary

- polygon
- attribute
- hexagon
- rhombus
- square
- triangle
- trapezoid

Talk like a mathematician:

The attributes of a _____ are _____.
(shape)

A _____ is a polygon because _____.
(shape)

One way a _____ and a _____ are
(shape)   (shape)
the same is _____.

Name: _____

My Polygon Picture

Write the number of blocks you used.

triangles _____   rhombuses _____   trapezoids _____

hexagons _____   squares _____

Number sentence: _____

Describe the attributes of your polygons.

1. _____

_____

2. _____

_____

3. _____

_____

You Write the Story

Materials

- *You Write the Story Cards* (pages 50–51)

- *My Story* recording sheet (page 52)

*.The *Talking Points* card and these reproducibles are also provided in the Digital Resources (story.pdf).

Overview

Students write, represent, and solve math stories to match equations.

Objective

Represent and solve problems involving addition and subtraction.

Procedure

Note: Prior to the lesson, copy the *You Write the Story Cards* (pages 50–51) on cardstock, cut, and laminate. A blank template is included to create cards for any type of equation (e.g., addition or subtraction).

1. Distribute copies of the *My Story* recording sheet (page 52) and other materials to students.

2. Students choose a card and do the following:

   - Write a math story based on the equation shown on the card.

   - Draw a math picture or diagram to represent the story.

   - Solve for the unknown number in the equation.

3. You may choose to have students show their thinking in their math journals or on their *My Story* recording sheets.

Differentiation

This activity may be easily differentiated by changing the equations that you use.

You Write the Story

Write a math story to match an equation.

You Write the Story

42 + 23 = ☐

You Write the Story

☐ + 16 = 52

Materials

- *You Write the Story Cards*
- *My Story* recording sheet

Directions

1. Choose a *You Write the Story Card*.

2. Write a math story that matches the equation. (Make sure the numbers make sense in your story.)

3. Draw a math picture or diagram that tells about your story.

4. Solve for the missing number in the equation.

Talking Points

Vocabulary

- sum
- difference
- addend
- equation
- diagram
- represent

Talk like a mathematician:

I organized my thinking by _____.

The numbers are reasonable in my story because _____.

My picture represents my equation because _____.

I can check my solution by _____.

Another way to solve this problem is _____.

Talking Points

Vocabulary

- sum
- difference
- addend
- equation
- diagram
- represent

Talk like a mathematician:

I organized my thinking by _____.

The numbers are reasonable in my story because _____.

My picture represents my equation because _____.

I can check my solution by _____.

Another way to solve this problem is _____.

You Write the Story Cards

You Write the Story

$$42 + 23 = \boxed{}$$

You Write the Story

$$38 + \boxed{} = 52$$

You Write the Story

$$\boxed{} + 16 = 52$$

You Write the Story

$$73 - 26 = \boxed{}$$

You Write the Story

$$85 - \boxed{} = 37$$

You Write the Story

$$\boxed{} - 28 = 14$$

You Write the Story Cards *(cont.)*

You Write the Story	**You Write the Story**
You Write the Story	**You Write the Story**
You Write the Story	**You Write the Story**

Name: _____

My Story

Directions: Write a math story that matches your equation. Draw a math picture or a diagram that shows your story.

_____

_____

_____

_____

_____

3. The missing number is _____ .

Using What We Know

What Is the Question?

Overview

Students use data from tables and graphs to write and solve questions.

Materials

- *What Is the Question? Cards* (pages 56–58)

- *What Is the Question?* recording sheet (page 59)

* The *Talking Points* card and these reproducibles are also provided in the Digital Resources (question.pdf).

Objective

Solve simple join, separate, and compare problems using information presented in graphs and tables.

Procedure

Note: Prior to introducing the workstation task, copy the *What Is the Question? Cards* (pages 56–58) on cardstock, cut, and laminate.

1. Distribute the *What Is the Question?* recording sheet (page 59) to students. Assign or have students select a question card.

2. Students read the card and write what they notice and wonder about the data.

3. Students write and answer two questions about the data.

Differentiation

- Students will choose numbers from the graph or table within their comfort zone, and will write more or less complicated questions, making this task self-differentiating.

- Provide **below-level-learners** with questions to solve, rather than having them write their own.

- Consider having students collect their own data and make graphs or tables to use in their workstations.

What Is the Question?

Write and solve questions using data from graphs and tables.

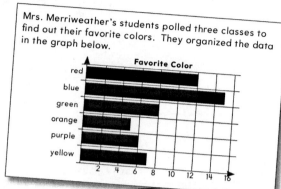

Mrs. Merriweather's students polled three classes to find out their favorite colors. They organized the data in the graph below.

Materials

- *What Is the Question? Cards*
- *What Is the Question?* recording sheet

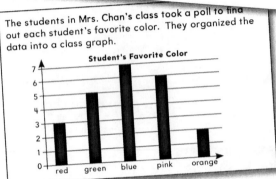

The students in Mrs. Chan's class took a poll to find out each student's favorite color. They organized the data into a class graph.

Directions

1. Look carefully at the graph or table on your card.

2. Make a list of things you notice and wonder about the data in your graph or table.

3. Turn two of the things you wonder about into math questions that can be answered using the data in the graph or table.

4. Solve your math questions.

Talking Points

Vocabulary
• table
• column
• row
• graph
• pictograph
• data

Talk like a mathematician:

Organizing data in a graph or table helps me because _____.

I noticed _____.

I wonder _____.

Labels are important on graphs and tables because _____.

Tables and graphs help mathematicians communicate effectively by _____.

Talking Points

Vocabulary
• table
• column
• row
• graph
• pictograph
• data

Talk like a mathematician:

Organizing data in a graph or table helps me because _____.

I noticed _____.

I wonder _____.

Labels are important on graphs and tables because _____.

Tables and graphs help mathematicians communicate effectively by _____.

What Is the Question? Cards

The students in Mrs. Chan's class took a poll to find out each student's favorite color. They organized the data in a graph.

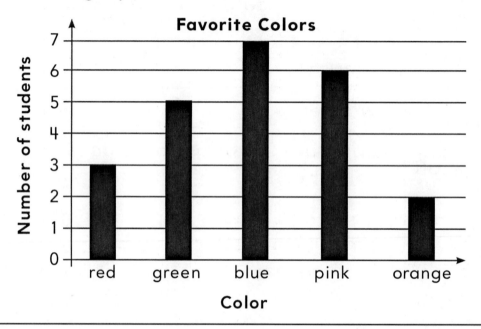

Martin Elementary School sold school supplies to raise money for playground equipment. The table shows the number of items sold each day of the sale.

Item	Wednesday	Thursday	Friday
pencils	120	104	117
erasers	87	101	75
pencil bags	28	19	32
magnets	56	67	58
notepads	34	43	36

What Is the Question? Cards *(cont.)*

For her birthday, Missy had a breakfast party at a bakery. The graph shows the items Missy and her friends ordered.

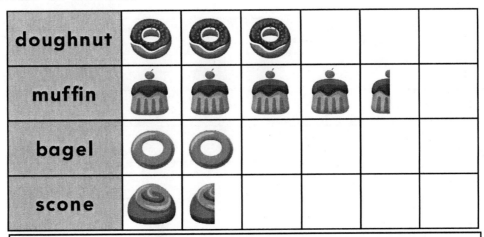

doughnut						
muffin						
bagel						
scone						

🍩 = 2   🧁 = 2   ⭕ = 2   🌀 = 2

Mrs. Merriweather's students surveyed three classes to find out their favorite colors. They organized the data in a graph.

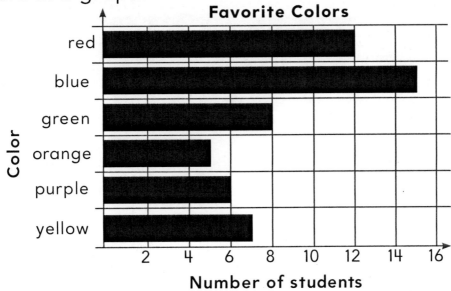

Favorite Colors

Number of students

Color

What Is the Question? Cards *(cont.)*

Chris read about animals in Africa. He read how fast they run and how much they weigh. Then, he organized the data in a table.

Animal	Speed (mph)	Average Weight (lbs.)
lion	50	350
cheetah	70	128
giraffe	32	2,200
ostrich	40	235
elephant	25	5,500

Juan's family went on a trip to visit his grandma. They kept track of the money they spent on food and gas.

	Friday	Saturday	Sunday	Monday
food	$85	$128	$102	$97
gas	$28	$32	$53	$29

Name: _____

What Is the Question?

Notice	Wonder

Question: _____

_____

Answer: _____

_____

Question: _____

_____

Answer: _____

_____

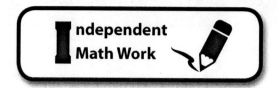

Representing Numbers

Materials

- *Representing Numbers Cards* (pages 63–65)

- *Representing Numbers* recording sheet (page 66)

- *Alternate Representing Numbers* recording sheet (page 67) (optional)

- base-ten blocks (optional)

* The *Talking Points* card and these reproducibles are also provided in the Digital Resources (representing.pdf).

Overview

Students write numbers as numerals, draw visual representations, and decompose numbers by place value.

Objective

Represent numbers to 120 in standard form, pictorial form, and expanded form.

Procedure

Note: Prior to the lesson, copy the *Representing Numbers Cards* (pages 63–65) on cardstock, cut, and laminate.

1. Distribute materials to students.

2. Students choose a card and write the number shown in the appropriate column on the *Representing Numbers* recording sheet (page 66).

3. Students write two other forms of the same number.

4. You may collect students' recording sheets or have students glue them in their math journals.

Differentiation

- Provide base-ten blocks for **below-level learners** who would benefit from the concrete experience of building the numbers.

- Choose cards appropriate to student needs. For example, a student might only work with cards showing numbers to 50.

- Challenge **above-level learners** to write numbers from least to greatest or greatest to least.

- Challenge **above-level learners** with the *Alternate Representing Numbers* recording sheet (page 67). Have them draw pictures showing the number two ways.

Representing Numbers

Represent numbers to 120 in standard form, expanded form, and as a picture.

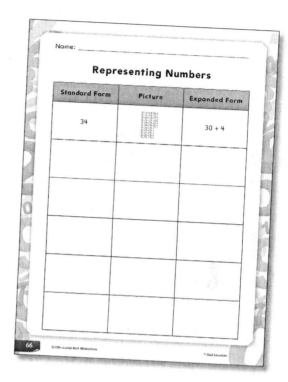

Materials

- *Representing Numbers Cards*
- *Representing Numbers* recording sheet
- base-ten blocks (optional)

Directions

1. Choose a card.

2. Write the number shown on your card in the matching column on your *Representing Numbers* recording sheet.

3. Write the two other forms of the same number. For example, if your card shows 34, write it in the Standard Form column. Then, write the number in expanded form and draw a picture.

4. Repeat with another card.

Talking Points

Vocabulary

- place value
- hundreds
- tens
- ones
- standard form
- expanded form

Talk like a mathematician:

My number has _____ hundreds, _____ tens, and _____ ones.

A ten is the same as _____ ones.

My number has _____ tens. The value of the tens is _____.

It is important to be able to represent numbers in more than one way because _____.

Talking Points

Vocabulary

- place value
- hundreds
- tens
- ones
- standard form
- expanded form

Talk like a mathematician:

My number has _____ hundreds, _____ tens, and _____ ones.

A ten is the same as _____ ones.

My number has _____ tens. The value of the tens is _____.

It is important to be able to represent numbers in more than one way because _____.

Representing Numbers Cards

18	25	37
42	59	65
71	86	93
110	115	10 + 5

Representing Numbers Cards *(cont.)*

20 + 3	**30 + 3**	**40 + 5**
50 + 4	**60 + 8**	**70 + 7**
80 + 2	**90 + 5**	**100 + 6**
100 + 10 + 2	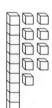	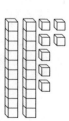

Representing Numbers Cards *(cont.)*

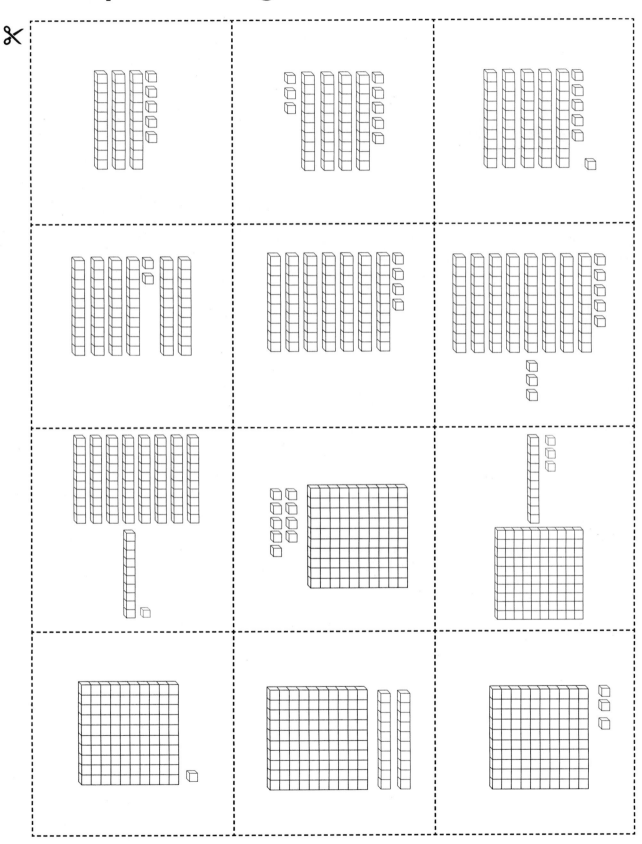

Representing Numbers

Standard Form	Picture	Expanded Form
34		30 + 4

Alternate Representing Numbers

Standard Form	Picture		Expanded Form
34			30 + 4

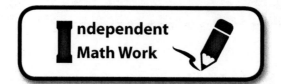

Independent Math Work

Missing Number Puzzles

Materials

- *120 Chart Puzzle* (page 71)

- *What's Missing?* recording sheet (page 72)

- *Reflect Like a Mathematician* recording sheet (page 73)

* The *Talking Points* card and these reproducibles are also provided in the Digital Resources (missing.pdf).

Overview

Students use the patterns in a 120 Chart to fit puzzle pieces together to form a complete chart.

Objective

Use place value understanding and properties of addition to add and subtract.

Procedure

Note: Prior to the lesson, copy the *120 Chart Puzzle* (page 71) on cardstock and laminate. Cut the chart into pieces, making sure that all the pieces contain some clue numbers. If making multiple puzzles, copy the activity sheet onto different colors of cardstock to identify the pieces for each set.

1. Distribute materials to students.

2. Students lay all of their puzzle pieces faceup and look for patterns to match the pieces.

3. Students put the puzzle pieces together to rebuild the *120 Chart Puzzle*.

4. Students may write the missing numbers on the *What's Missing?* recording sheet (page 72) as a record of their work.

5. Students may complete the *Reflect Like a Mathematician* recording sheet (page 73) to describe patterns found in the *120 Chart Puzzle*.

Differentiation

- For **below-level learners**, you may choose to cut a completed *120 Chart*, rather than the partially completed chart. You may also choose to cut the chart into fewer pieces.

- Challenge **above-level learners** with charts containing numbers above 120.

Missing Number Puzzles

Arrange puzzle pieces to create a complete 120 Chart.

Materials

- *120 Chart Puzzle*
- *What's Missing?* recording sheet
- *Reflect Like a Mathematician* recording sheet

What's Missing?

1	2		4	5			8	9	10
	12	13		15				19	20
21				25		27			30
31		33				37			
			44						50
51		53		55			58		
			64				68		
71					76				
	82	83						89	
				95	96			99	100
		103				107			
111				115				119	120

Directions

1. Place all of the puzzle pieces faceup.

2. Look carefully at the numbers on your puzzle pieces. Look for patterns that will help you match the pieces.

3. Put the puzzle pieces together to make a completed 120 Chart.

4. Write the missing numbers on the *What's Missing?* recording sheet.

5. Write about the patterns you found on the *Reflect Like a Mathematician* recording sheet.

Talking Points

Vocabulary

- ten more ↓
- ten less ↑
- one more →
- one less ←
- column
- row
- pattern

Talk like a mathematician:

The _____ fits here because _____.

I can find a number that is 10 more than _____ by _____.

My strategy for matching pieces is _____.

A pattern I see on the chart is _____.

Talking Points

Vocabulary

- ten more ↓
- ten less ↑
- one more →
- one less ←
- column
- row
- pattern

Talk like a mathematician:

The _____ fits here because _____.

I can find a number that is 10 more than _____ by _____.

My strategy for matching pieces is _____.

A pattern I see on the chart is _____.

120 Chart Puzzle

1	2	3	4	5	6	7	8	9	10
11	12	13	14	15	16	17	18	19	20
21	22	23	24	25	26	27	28	29	30
31	32	33	34	35	36	37	38	39	40
41	42	43	44	45	46	47	48	49	50
51	52	53	54	55	56	57	58	59	60
61	62	63	64	65	66	67	68	69	70
71	72	73	74	75	76	77	78	79	80
81	82	83	84	85	86	87	88	89	90
91	92	93	94	95	96	97	98	99	100
101	102	103	104	105	106	107	108	109	110
111	112	113	114	115	116	117	118	119	120

What's Missing?

1	2		4	5			8	9	10
	12	13		15				19	20
21				25		27			30
31		33				37			
			44						50
51		53		55			58		
			64				68		
71					76				
	82	83						89	
				95	96			99	100
		103				107			
111				115				119	120

51728—Guided Math Workstations

Name: _____

Reflect Like a Mathematician

Directions: What patterns do you see in the 120 Chart? Why is this important? Explain using words and pictures.

1	2	3	4	5	6	7	8	9	10
11	12	13	14	15	16	17	18	19	20
21	22	23	24	25	26	27	28	29	30

row ➡ (row 2)

column (points to 28)

_____

_____

_____

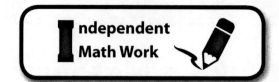

Piggy Bank Problems

Overview

Students draw five cards and find the value of the collection of coins shown on the cards.

Objective

Find the value of a collection of coins.

Procedure

Note: Prior to introducing the workstation task, copy the *Piggy Bank Problems Cards* (page 77) on cardstock, cut, and laminate.

1. Distribute copies of the *What's the Value?* recording sheets (pages 78–79) and other materials to students.

2. Students draw five cards, arrange them by coin type from greatest value to least value, and find the value of the coins. Using one set of cards, the value of the collection will always be under one dollar. Students may use play money or the *120 Chart* (page 81) to help them count.

3. Students record the five coins from the cards and the value of the collection, using both the cent symbol and a dollar sign and decimal point, on the *What's the Value?* recording sheets.

4. Students continue with five more cards, reshuffling and reusing the cards as needed.

5. You may collect students' recording sheets or have students glue them in their math journals.

Differentiation

- Copy the *Coin Value Chart* (page 80) on cardstock, cut, and laminate. Have **below-level learners** who need support lay the coin value pieces over the *120 Chart* to determine the value of the collection.

- Challenge **above-level learners** with the following ideas:

  - Make several copies of the cards and allow students to draw more cards, creating the possibility of collections over one dollar.

  - Have students find one or more additional ways to create the same value using different coins.

  - Have students list the values of their coin collections from least to greatest or greatest to least.

Materials

- *Piggy Bank Problems Cards* (page 77)

- *What's the Value?* recording sheet (pages 78–79)

- *Coin Value Chart* (page 80) (optional)

- play coins (optional)

- *120 Chart* (page 81) (optional)

* The *Talking Points* card and these reproducibles are also provided in the Digital Resources (piggybank.pdf).

Piggy Bank Problems

Find the value of a collection of coins.

Materials

- *Piggy Bank Problems Cards*
- *What's the Value?* recording sheet
- *Coin Value Chart* (optional)
- play coins
- *120 Chart* (optional)

Directions

1. Shuffle the *Piggy Bank Problems Cards* and put them facedown in a pile.

2. Draw 5 cards.

3. Arrange the cards so like coins are together. Arrange the groups from greatest value to least value.

4. Find the value of the coins. Use play coins or the *120 Chart* to help you.

5. Show your thinking on the *What's the Value?* recording sheet.

Talking Points

Vocabulary

- quarter (25¢)
- dime (10¢)
- nickel (5¢)
- penny (1¢)
- cent
- value

Talk like a mathematician:

My strategy for finding the value of the coins is _____.

The value of my coins is _____.

Another way to show the same amount is _____.

I arranged my coins from greatest value to least value because _____.

Talking Points

Vocabulary

- quarter (25¢)
- dime (10¢)
- nickel (5¢)
- penny (1¢)
- cent
- value

Talk like a mathematician:

My strategy for finding the value of the coins is _____.

The value of my coins is _____.

Another way to show the same amount is _____.

I arranged my coins from greatest value to least value because _____.

Piggy Bank Problems Cards

What's the Value?

Directions: Label the coins to show the cards you drew. Write the value with the cent symbol. Write the value with a dollar sign and decimal point.

Coins	Cent Symbol	Dollar Sign and Decimal Point
Q Q D N P	66¢	$0.66
◯ ◯ ◯ ◯ ◯		
◯ ◯ ◯ ◯ ◯		
◯ ◯ ◯ ◯ ◯		

What's the Value? *(cont.)*

Coins	Cent Symbol	Dollar Sign and Decimal Point

Coin Value Chart

quarter

quarter

quarter

	nickel
nickel	nickel

dime

dime

dime

p	p	p

51728—Guided Math Workstations © *Shell Education*

120 Chart

1	2	3	4	5	6	7	8	9	10
11	12	13	14	15	16	17	18	19	20
21	22	23	24	25	26	27	28	29	30
31	32	33	34	35	36	37	38	39	40
41	42	43	44	45	46	47	48	49	50
51	52	53	54	55	56	57	58	59	60
61	62	63	64	65	66	67	68	69	70
71	72	73	74	75	76	77	78	79	80
81	82	83	84	85	86	87	88	89	90
91	92	93	94	95	96	97	98	99	100
101	102	103	104	105	106	107	108	109	110
111	112	113	114	115	116	117	118	119	120

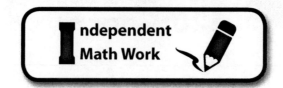

Numberless Word Problems

- -

Overview

Students choose numbers to use in a word problem, draw a picture representing the problem, and solve it.

- -

Objective

Use addition and subtraction to solve word problems involving situations of joining, separating, part-part-whole, and comparing, with unknowns in any position.

Procedure

Note: Prior to introducing the workstation activity sheets, copy the *Numberless Word Problems* (pages 85–89) and cut apart. You may choose to select one problem for all students to complete or provide several and allow students to choose.

1. Students glue their problems on copies of the *Missing Numbers* recording sheet (page 90).

2. Students choose their own numbers to complete the word problem, draw a picture representing the problem, and solve it. Encourage students to write their answers using complete sentences. (e.g., How many pencils did Marla have to begin with? Marla had _____ pencils to begin with.)

Differentiation

- This task is self-differentiating because students will choose numbers they are comfortable working with. Consider providing a range of numbers for students to use to prevent them from using numbers that are either too easy or too challenging.

- Provide manipulatives or props to **below-level learners** who might benefit from acting out the problems.

- Challenge **above-level learners** to represent the problems in more than one way (e.g., picture and number line).

Materials

- *Numberless Word Problems* (pages 85–89)

- *Missing Numbers* recording sheet (optional) (page 90)

- manipulatives

* The *Talking Points* card and these reproducibles are also provided in the Digital Resources (numberless.pdf).

Numberless Word Problems

Choose numbers to complete a word problem. Draw a picture to represent the problem and solve it.

> There are _____ puppies and _____ kittens at the pet store. How many animals are at the pet store?
>
> How many more kittens are at the pet store

> Marla had some pencils. Stephanie gave her _____ more pencils. Now Marla has _____ pencils.
> How many pencils did Marla have to begin with?

Materials

- *Numberless Word Problems*
- *Missing Numbers* recording sheet
- manipulatives

Directions

1. Glue your problem on the *Missing Numbers* recording sheet.

2. Read your problem very carefully to make sure you understand the story.

3. Try different numbers in the blanks, and act out the story with manipulatives.

4. Choose the numbers that make the most sense. Write them on the blank lines.

5. Draw a picture that matches your math story.

6. Solve the problem. Then, write your answer in a complete sentence. Think about your solution and be sure it makes sense.

Talking Points

Vocabulary
- add
- subtract
- join
- separate
- compare
- fewer
- more
- altogether

Talk like a mathematician:

This story reminds me of _____.

My solution makes sense because _____.

Manipulatives helped because _____.

Drawing a picture helped me _____.

My picture matches the word problem because _____.

Talking Points

Vocabulary
- add
- subtract
- join
- separate
- compare
- fewer
- more
- altogether

Talk like a mathematician:

This story reminds me of _____.

My solution makes sense because _____.

Manipulatives helped because _____.

Drawing a picture helped me _____.

My picture matches the word problem because _____.

Numberless Word Problems

There are _____ puppies and _____ kittens at the pet store. How many animals are at the pet store?
How many more kittens are at the pet store than puppies?

Marla had some pencils. Stephanie gave her _____ more pencils. Now Marla has _____ pencils.
How many pencils did Marla have to begin with?

Numberless Word Problems *(cont.)*

There are _____ fewer boys than girls in Ms. Mack's class. There are _____ boys. How many girls are in Ms. Mack's class?

How many students are in Ms. Mack's class altogether?

There were some squirrels playing in the tree. _____ squirrels ran away. Now there are _____ squirrels in the tree. How many squirrels were in the tree at first?

51728—Guided Math Workstations

Numberless Word Problems *(cont.)*

There are _____ more tall-tale books on the shelf than fairy tale books. There are _____ fairy tale books. How many tall-tale books are on the shelf? How many books are on the shelf altogether?

Mrs. Walton bought _____ apples and some oranges at the grocery store. She bought _____ pieces of fruit in total. How many oranges did Mrs. Walton buy? How many more apples did Mrs. Walton buy than oranges?

Numberless Word Problems *(cont.)*

There were _____ tomatoes in Mr. Key's garden. He picked some tomatoes to use for dinner. Now there are _____ tomatoes in Mr. Key's garden. How many tomatoes did Mr. Key pick?

Marcus had _____ pieces of candy. He gave _____ pieces of candy to his sister. How many pieces of candy does Marcus have left?

Alex had _____ coins. His mom gave him _____ more coins. How many coins does Alex have now?

Numberless Word Problems (cont.)

Robert had _____ stickers on his reward chart. His teacher gave him some more stickers. Now he has _____ stickers on his reward chart. How many stickers did Robert's teacher give him?

Luke has _____ more rocks in his rock collection than Joseph. Joseph has _____ rocks in his collection. How many rocks does Luke have in his rock collection?

Nancy made _____ bracelets and some necklaces. She made _____ pieces of jewelry altogether. How many necklaces did Nancy make?

Name: _____

Missing Numbers

Directions: Glue your word problem in the box. Choose numbers that make sense for the story. Draw a picture to solve the problem.

Number Sentence: _____

Make 5, Capture 4

Overview

Students cover pairs of numbers that make 5 and try to claim four squares in a row.

Objective

Fluently add and subtract within 10.

Procedure

Note: Prior to the lesson, copy the *Make 5, Capture 4 Game Board* (page 94) on cardstock and laminate, or place in a sheet protector. Use the *Game Board Template* (page 95) to create game boards with combinations for other numbers. For example, create a game board with pairs of numbers to make 6 or 7.

1. Distribute materials to students.

2. Students take turns choosing a pair of numbers that make 5, stating their combination (e.g., 1 and 4 make 5), and covering the spaces with their counters. Two-color counters work well, with each player using a different color. Students may also use dry-erase markers and mark their spaces with *X*s and *O*s.

3. The first player to claim 4 spaces in a row horizontally, vertically, or diagonally wins.

4. Students may record the combinations for 5 either in their math journals or on the *I Made 5* recording sheet (page 96).

Differentiation

- Provide manipulatives to **below-level learners** who need concrete support for determining combinations.

- Challenge **above-level learners** to use more than two addends to make the target number.

Materials

- *Make 5, Capture 4 Game Board* (page 94)

- *Game Board Template* (page 95)

- colored counters or dry-erase markers

- *I Made 5* recording sheet (optional) (page 96)

* The *Talking Points* card and these reproducibles are also provided in the Digital Resources (make5.pdf).

Make 5, Capture 4

Choose number pairs that make 5. Capture 4 spaces in a row to win!

Make 5, Capture 4 Game Board

Materials

- *Make 5, Capture 4 Game Board*
- colored counters for each player or dry-erase markers
- *I Made 5* recording sheet (optional)

Directions

1. Choose which player will go first.

2. Take turns:

   - Find 2 spaces with numbers that make 5.
   - Say the combination.
   - Mark the 2 spaces.

3. Mark 4 spaces in a row first to win!

Talking Points

Vocabulary	Talk like a mathematician:

Vocabulary

- compose
- combination
- number pair
- add
- addition
- addend
- sum
- strategy

Talk like a mathematician:

Five is the sum of _____ and _____.

_____ plus _____ equals _____.

If I have _____, I need _____ more to make _____.

The strategy I use to choose my spaces is _____.

✂ -

Talking Points

Vocabulary

- compose
- combination
- number pair
- add
- addition
- addend
- sum
- strategy

Talk like a mathematician:

Five is the sum of _____ and _____.

_____ plus _____ equals _____.

If I have _____, I need _____ more to make _____.

The strategy I use to choose my spaces is _____.

Make 5, Capture 4 Game Board

(fist)	(die: 4)	**3**	(die: 5)
(die: 1)	(hand: 5)	**2**	**0**
1	(die: 3)	(hand: 1 finger)	(hand: 2 fingers)
(hand: 3 fingers)	**5**	(die: 2)	**4**

Game Board Template

Make _____, Capture _____

Name: _____

I Made 5

_____ + _____ = 5

_____ + _____ = 5

_____ + _____ = 5

_____ + _____ = 5

_____ + _____ = 5

_____ + _____ = 5

_____ + _____ = 5

Developing Fluency

Make 10, Capture 4

Overview

Students cover pairs of numbers that make 10 and try to claim four squares in a row.

Materials

- *Make 10, Capture 4 Game Board* (page 100)

- *Game Board Template* (page 101)

- colored counters or dry-erase markers

- *I Made 10* recording sheet (optional) (page 102)

* The *Talking Points* card and these reproducibles are also provided in the Digital Resources (make10.pdf).

Objective

For any number 1–9, find the number that makes 10 when added to the given number.

Procedure

Note: Prior to the lesson, copy the *Make 10, Capture 4 Game Board* (page 100) on cardstock and laminate, or place in a sheet protector. Use the *Game Board Template* (page 101) to create game boards with combinations of other numbers. For example, create a game board with pairs of numbers to make 6 or 7.

1. Distribute materials to students.

2. Students take turns choosing a pair of numbers that make 10, stating their combination (e.g., 2 and 8 make 10), and covering the spaces with their counters. Two-color counters work well with each player using a different color. Students may also use dry-erase markers and mark their spaces with *X*s and *O*s.

3. The first player to claim 4 spaces in a row horizontally, vertically, or diagonally wins.

4. Students may record the combinations for 10 either in their math journals or on the *I Made 10* recording sheet (page 102).

Differentiation

- Provide manipulatives to **below-level learners** who need concrete support for determining combinations.

- Challenge **above-level learners** to use more than two addends to make the target number.

Make 10, Capture 4

Choose number pairs that make 10. Capture 4 spaces in a row to win!

Make 10, Capture 4 Game Board

Materials

- *Make 10, Capture 4 Game Board*
- colored counters for each player or dry-erase markers
- *I Made 10* recording sheet

Directions

1. Choose which player will go first.

2. Take turns:

   - Find 2 spaces with numbers that make 10.
   - Say the combination.
   - Mark the 2 spaces.

3. Mark 4 spaces in a row first to win!

Talking Points

Vocabulary	**Talk like a mathematician:**

Vocabulary

- compose
- combination
- number pair
- add
- addition
- addend
- sum
- strategy

Talk like a mathematician:

Ten is the sum of _____ and _____.

_____ plus _____ equals _____.

If I have _____, I need _____ more to make _____.

The strategy I use to choose my spaces is _____.

✂ -

Talking Points

Vocabulary

- compose
- combination
- number pair
- add
- addition
- addend
- sum
- strategy

Talk like a mathematician:

Ten is the sum of _____ and _____.

_____ plus _____ equals _____.

If I have _____, I need _____ more to make _____.

The strategy I use to choose my spaces is _____.

Make 10, Capture 4 Game Board

✊	eight	**3**	🎲 (5)	**6**
🎲 (1)	✋	(ten frame, full)	🤟 (3 fingers)	**9**
1	🎲 (3)	nine	✌️ (2 fingers)	(ten frame, 5)
(ten frame)	**5**	🎲 (2)	**4**	zero
five	🎲 (6)	**7**	**10**	**8**

Game Board Template

Make _____, Capture _____

I Made 10

_____ + _____ = 10

_____ + _____ = 10

_____ + _____ = 10

_____ + _____ = 10

_____ + _____ = 10

_____ + _____ = 10

_____ + _____ = 10

Addition Move One

Overview

Students change one addend to capture a space on the game board. The first player to get four in a row wins.

Materials

- *Addition Move One Game Board* (page 106)

- 2 paper clips

- dry-erase markers

- *Addition/Subtraction Chart* (optional) (page 107)

* The *Talking Points* card and these reproducibles are also provided in the Digital Resources (moveone.pdf).

Objective

Add and subtract within 20 using mental strategies.

Procedure

Note: Prior to introducing the workstation task, copy the *Addition Move One Game Board* (page 106) on cardstock (one game board per student pair) and laminate, or place in a sheet protector.

1. Distribute materials to students.

2. Player 1 places the paper clips on two addends at the bottom of the game board, adds to find the sum, and marks a space with the sum on the game board.

3. Player 2 moves only one paper clip to a different addend, adds, and marks a space with the sum on the game board. Both paper clips may be placed on the same addend (e.g., 3 and 3).

4. Players may use *X*s and *O*s to differentiate their marks or colored game markers. The first player to claim four spaces in a row wins.

5. Students may record the facts from each of their turns in their math journals. Or, students may make brief videos explaining their strategies and reflecting on changes they might try when playing the game again.

Differentiation

- Some players are using the game to build automaticity, while others are playing to learn their math facts. Include an *Addition/Subtraction Chart* (page 107), and encourage students to use the chart rather than guess at a math fact they do not know.

- Create a game board with fewer addends for **below-level learners**. For example, create a game board with the addends 0, 1, 2, 3, 4, and 5 to practice only math facts to 5.

- Have **above-level learners** combine three addends using three paper clips.

Addition Move One

Choose addends to mark four spaces in a row on the game board.

Materials

- *Addition Move One Game Board*
- 2 paper clips
- dry-erase markers
- *Addition/Subtraction Chart* (optional)
- manipulatives (optional)

Addition Move One Game Board

11	18	7	13	8	5	10	16
9	5	12	16	18	14	9	17
8	10	14	6	11	12	13	6
14	11	15	10	15	8	16	11
6	13	9	14	17	12	5	17
17	10	16	5	7	15	16	12
7	14	12	15	18	6	9	18
13	7	18	8	11	17	15	10

2 3 4 5 6 7 8 9

Directions

1. Choose which player will go first.

2. Take Turns

- **Player 1:** Place the paper clips on two addends at the bottom of the game board. (Both paper clips may be placed on the same addend.) Add to find the sum. Mark a space with that sum on the game board.
- **Player 2:** Move one paper clip to a different addend. Add to find the sum. Mark a space with that sum on the game board.

3. Mark four spaces in a row to win!

Talking Points

Vocabulary	Talk like a mathematician:

Vocabulary
- addend
- sum
- plus
- add
- addition
- double

Talk like a mathematician:

I marked the sum _____ because _____ plus _____ equals _____.

_____ is the sum of _____ and _____.

The addends I chose are _____ and _____ because they have a sum of _____.

The strategy I used to choose my addends is _____.

Talking Points

Vocabulary
- addend
- sum
- plus
- add
- addition
- double

Talk like a mathematician:

I marked the sum _____ because _____ plus _____ equals _____.

_____ is the sum of _____ and _____.

The addends I chose are _____ and _____ because they have a sum of _____.

The strategy I used to choose my addends is _____.

Addition Move One Game Board

11	18	7	13	8	5	10	16
9	5	12	16	18	14	9	17
8	10	14	6	11	12	13	6
14	11	15	10	15	8	16	11
6	13	9	14	17	12	5	17
17	10	16	5	7	15	16	12
7	14	12	15	18	6	9	18
13	7	18	8	11	17	15	10

2 3 4 5 6 7 8 9

Addition/Subtraction Chart

+/−	1	2	3	4	5	6	7	8	9	10
1	2	3	4	5	6	7	8	9	10	11
2	3	4	5	6	7	8	9	10	11	12
3	4	5	6	7	8	9	10	11	12	13
4	5	6	7	8	9	10	11	12	13	14
5	6	7	8	9	10	11	12	13	14	15
6	7	8	9	10	11	12	13	14	15	16
7	8	9	10	11	12	13	14	15	16	17
8	9	10	11	12	13	14	15	16	17	18
9	10	11	12	13	14	15	16	17	18	19
10	11	12	13	14	15	16	17	18	19	20

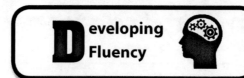

Sum or Difference

Overview

Students earn points by having the greatest sum or difference of two numbers.

Objective

Add and subtract within 100.

Procedure

Note: Prior to the lesson, copy the *Numbers to 100 Cards* (pages 111–117) on cardstock, cut, and laminate. To keep the sums within 100, only put cards from 1–50 in the workstation.

1. Distribute materials to students.

2. Players shuffle the cards and place them facedown in a pile.

3. Each player takes two cards from the pile and places them faceup.

4. Players estimate both the sum and difference of their numbers and predict who will have the greater sum or difference using copies of the *Sum or Difference* recording sheet (page 118).

5. Players roll the number cube to determine whether they will add or subtract. If an even number is rolled, they will add. If an odd number is rolled, they will subtract.

6. Players perform their calculations and then compare their sums or differences. The player with the greatest sum or difference takes all the cards.

7. The player with the most cards at the end of the game wins.

8. You may collect students' recording sheets or have students glue them in their math journals.

Differentiation

- For **below-level learners**, limit the numbers on the cards to those they are comfortable with.

- For **above-level learners**, extend the number cards to three-digit numbers.

- Provide copies of an *Addition/Subtraction Chart* (page 119) or manipulatives to students who still need concrete support.

Materials

- *Numbers to 100 Cards* (pages 111–117)

- *Sum or Difference* recording sheet (page 118)

- number cube

- *Addition/Subtraction Chart* (optional) (page 119)

- manipulatives (optional)

* The *Talking Points* card and these reproducibles are also provided in the Digital Resources (sumordiff.pdf).

Sum or Difference

Earn points by having the greatest sum or difference of 2 numbers.

Materials

- *Numbers to 100 Cards*
- *Sum or Difference* recording sheet
- number cube

Directions

1. Shuffle the cards. Place them facedown in a pile.

2. Each player takes 2 cards from the top of the pile. Turn them faceup.

3. Estimate both the sum and difference of your numbers. Predict who will have the greater sum or difference. Write your estimates on the *Sum or Difference* recording sheet.

4. Roll the number cube. If the number rolled is even, find the sum of the numbers on the cards. If the number rolled is odd, find the difference of the numbers on the cards.

5. The player with the greatest sum or difference keeps the cards. The player with the most cards at the end of the game wins.

Talking Points

Vocabulary
• sum
• difference
• addend
• estimate
• greater than
• less than
• odd
• even

Talk like a mathematician:

I estimated by _____.

I know _____ is even/odd because _____.

My strategy to add/subtract is _____.

The sum of my numbers is _____.

The difference between my numbers is _____.

_____ is greater than _____ because _____.

✂ -

Talking Points

Vocabulary
• sum
• difference
• addend
• estimate
• greater than
• less than
• odd
• even

Talk like a mathematician:

I estimated by _____.

I know _____ is even/odd because _____.

My strategy to add/subtract is _____.

The sum of my numbers is _____.

The difference between my numbers is _____.

_____ is greater than _____ because _____.

Numbers to 100 Cards

1	2	3
4	5	6
7	8	9
10	11	12
13	14	15

Numbers to 100 Cards *(cont.)*

16	17	18
19	20	21
22	23	24
25	26	27
28	29	30

51728—Guided Math Workstations

Numbers to 100 Cards *(cont.)*

31	32	33
34	35	36
37	38	39
40	41	42
43	44	45

Numbers to 100 Cards *(cont.)*

46	47	48
49	50	51
52	53	54
55	56	57
58	59	60

Numbers to 100 Cards (cont.)

61	62	63
64	65	66
67	68	69
70	71	72
73	74	75

Numbers to 100 Cards *(cont.)*

76	77	78
79	80	81
82	83	84
85	86	87
88	89	90

Numbers to 100 Cards *(cont.)*

91	92	93
94	95	96
97	98	99
100		

Name: _____

Sum or Difference

Directions: Estimate the sum and difference. Then, find the actual sum or difference.

Estimate		Actual	
Sum	**Difference**	**Sum**	**Difference**
Sum	**Difference**	**Sum**	**Difference**
Sum	**Difference**	**Sum**	**Difference**
Sum	**Difference**	**Sum**	**Difference**

Addition/Subtraction Chart

+/−	1	2	3	4	5	6	7	8	9	10
1	2	3	4	5	6	7	8	9	10	11
2	3	4	5	6	7	8	9	10	11	12
3	4	5	6	7	8	9	10	11	12	13
4	5	6	7	8	9	10	11	12	13	14
5	6	7	8	9	10	11	12	13	14	15
6	7	8	9	10	11	12	13	14	15	16
7	8	9	10	11	12	13	14	15	16	17
8	9	10	11	12	13	14	15	16	17	18
9	10	11	12	13	14	15	16	17	18	19
10	11	12	13	14	15	16	17	18	19	20

Developing
Fluency

Par for the Course

- -

Overview

Players add and subtract numbers rolled on number cubes to compete on an 18-hole golf course. The player with the fewest strokes wins the game.

- -

Objective

Add and subtract to build automaticity with math facts.

Procedure

1. Distribute copies of the *Par for the Course* recording sheet (page 123) and other materials to students.

2. Each "hole" has a different objective. Player 1 rolls two number cubes as many times as necessary to meet the goal of each hole. For example, on Hole 1, students must roll a sum greater than 8. Each time the students roll, it counts as a stroke. The player must keep rolling until he or she meets the goal for that hole.

3. When the goal is met, Player 1 records his or her score and proof of score on the *Par for the Course* recording sheet. The score is the number of times the number cubes were rolled.

4. Player 2 repeats the process for Hole 1.

5. Play continues until all 18 holes have been played. The player with the lowest total score wins.

6. You may choose to collect students' recording sheets or have students glue them in their math journals.

Differentiation

- You may choose to provide **below-level learners** with concrete objects to represent each roll as a tracking strategy. Provide copies of the *Addition/Subtraction Chart* (page 124) or manipulatives to students who still need concrete support.

- Challenge **above-level learners** to work with larger numbers.

- Challenge **above-level learners** to determine what par should be for each hole, based on the probability of rolling numbers that meet the objective.

(Adapted from MathNook 2016)

Materials

- 2 number cubes

- *Par for the Course* recording sheet (page 123)

- *Addition/Subtraction Chart* (optional) (page 124)

- manipulatives (optional)

* The *Talking Points* card and these reproducibles are also provided in the Digital Resources (par.pdf).

Par for the Course

Meet the goal for each hole on this golf course with the fewest strokes possible.

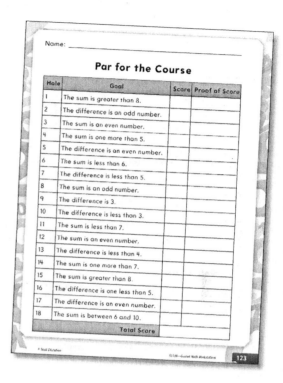

Materials

- 2 number cubes
- *Par for the Course* recording sheet

Directions

1. Take turns:

   - Roll the number cubes until you meet the goal. Each roll counts as one stroke. For example, if it takes you 7 rolls to meet the goal, your score is 7 for the hole.
   - When your roll meets the goal, write the number sentence showing how you met the goal in the Proof of Score column. Write how many strokes it took to meet the goal in the Score column.

2. Earn the lowest total score to win!

Talking Points

Vocabulary

- sum
- addend
- difference
- odd
- even
- greater than
- less than

Talk like a mathematician:

_____ is odd because _____.

_____ is even because _____.

The sum of my addends is _____.

The difference of my numbers is _____.

_____ is greater than _____ because _____.

_____ is less than _____ because _____.

Talking Points

Vocabulary

- sum
- addend
- difference
- odd
- even
- greater than
- less than

Talk like a mathematician:

_____ is odd because _____.

_____ is even because _____.

The sum of my addends is _____.

The difference of my numbers is _____.

_____ is greater than _____ because _____.

_____ is less than _____ because _____.

Name: _____

Par for the Course

Hole	Goal	Score	Proof of Score
1	The sum is greater than 8.		
2	The difference is an odd number.		
3	The sum is an even number.		
4	The sum is one more than 5.		
5	The difference is an even number.		
6	The sum is less than 6.		
7	The difference is less than 5.		
8	The sum is an odd number.		
9	The difference is 3.		
10	The difference is less than 3.		
11	The sum is less than 7.		
12	The sum is an even number.		
13	The difference is less than 4.		
14	The sum is one more than 7.		
15	The sum is greater than 8.		
16	The difference is one less than 5.		
17	The difference is an even number.		
18	The sum is between 6 and 10.		
	Total Score		

Addition/Subtraction Chart

+/−	1	2	3	4	5	6	7	8	9	10
1	2	3	4	5	6	7	8	9	10	11
2	3	4	5	6	7	8	9	10	11	12
3	4	5	6	7	8	9	10	11	12	13
4	5	6	7	8	9	10	11	12	13	14
5	6	7	8	9	10	11	12	13	14	15
6	7	8	9	10	11	12	13	14	15	16
7	8	9	10	11	12	13	14	15	16	17
8	9	10	11	12	13	14	15	16	17	18
9	10	11	12	13	14	15	16	17	18	19
10	11	12	13	14	15	16	17	18	19	20

51728—Guided Math Workstations

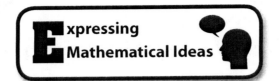

Math Vocabulary Book

Overview

Students define and illustrate math words in a personal vocabulary book.

Objective

Communicate precisely, using clear definitions when discussing and reasoning about mathematics.

Procedure

Note: Prior to introducing the workstation task, assemble a *Math Vocabulary Book* for each student. Each double-sided vocabulary page accommodates four words.

1. Distribute the copies of the *My Math Vocabulary Book* (pages 128–130) and other materials to students.

2. Students use the cover provided to create a math vocabulary book that may be used all year long, or they may create an alternate cover for topic-specific vocabulary books.

3. Students will either choose or be assigned a mathematical word.

4. Students complete a page of the book as follows:
   - **Word**—vocabulary word
   - **What It Means**—student definition of the word
   - **What It Looks Like**—drawing showing the vocabulary word

5. Consider having students record their definitions as audio files, generate QR codes or other digital representations, and glue the codes in their "What It Means" sections.

6. You may choose to collect students' vocabulary books as evidence of learning.

Differentiation

- Provide words and definitions that may be cut and pasted for **below-level learners** who struggle with writing and defining the vocabulary words. They may show their understanding of the words by creating illustrations or by using voice recorders to record the definitions in their own words.

- Have **above-level learners** create books using the *Alternate Math Vocabulary Book* (pages 131–133), which includes a "Reminds Me Of" section for making connections.

Materials

- *My Math Vocabulary Book* (pages 128–130)

- crayons or colored pencils (optional)

- Math Word Wall or list of vocabulary words

- digital device for recording an audio of the definition (optional)

- *Alternate Math Vocabulary Book* (pages 131–133)

* The *Talking Points* card and these reproducibles are also provided in the Digital Resources (vocabbook.pdf).

Math Vocabulary Book

Tell about words and show their meanings.

Materials

- *My Math Vocabulary Book*
- crayons or colored pencils (optional)

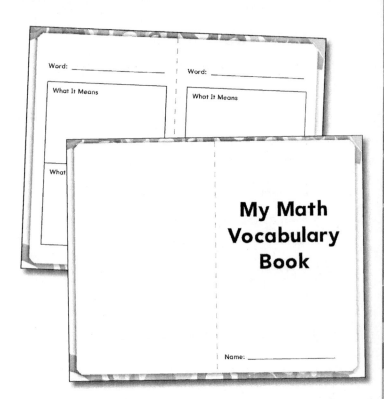

Directions

1. Think about what the math word means and what it looks like.

2. Turn to the next blank page in your book.

3. In each part of the chart:

   - **Word**—Write the math vocabulary word.
   - **What It Means**—Explain what the word means.
   - **What It Looks Like**—Draw a picture to show what your word means.

4. Remember to use precise mathematical language.

Talking Points

Vocabulary	Talk like a mathematician:

Vocabulary
- explain
- describe
- represent
- example
- non-example
- connection

Talk like a mathematician:

The word _____ means _____.

My picture represents _____.

The word _____ reminds me of _____.

An example of _____ is _____.

An non-example of _____ is _____.

I made a connection between _____ and _____ because _____.

✂ ┄┄┄┄┄┄┄┄┄┄┄┄┄┄┄┄┄┄┄┄┄┄┄┄┄┄┄┄┄┄┄┄┄┄┄┄┄┄

Talking Points

Vocabulary
- explain
- describe
- represent
- example
- non-example
- connection

Talk like a mathematician:

The word _____ means _____.

My picture represents _____.

The word _____ reminds me of _____.

An example of _____ is _____.

An non-example of _____ is _____.

I made a connection between _____ and _____ because _____.

My Math Vocabulary Book

Name: _____

Word: _____

What It Means	What It Looks Like

Word: _____

What It Means	What It Looks Like

Word: _____

What It Means	What It Looks Like

Word: _____

What It Means	What It Looks Like

Alternate Math Vocabulary Book

Name: _____

Word: _____

What It Means	What It Looks Like	Reminds Me Of...

Word: _____

What It Means	What It Looks Like	Reminds Me Of...

Word: _____

What It Means	**What It Looks Like**	**Reminds Me Of...**

Word: _____

What It Means	**What It Looks Like**	**Reminds Me Of...**

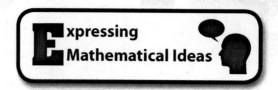

Survey Says...

- -

Overview

Students develop and conduct a survey, tally and graph the responses, and write statements to interpret the results.

- -

Materials

- *Survey Says* recording sheet (page 137)

- *My Graph* graphing sheet (page 138)

* The *Talking Points* card and these reproducibles are also provided in the Digital Resources (survey.pdf).

Objective

Organize, represent, and interpret data with up to three categories.

Procedure

1. Distribute materials to students.

2. Students choose a survey question with three responses. They write the question on their *Survey Says* recording sheet (page 137) and the three responses for the categories in the column headings of the tally chart.

3. Students survey other students in the class or in their group and record their responses in the tally chart.

4. Using the data from the tally chart, students create bar graphs by coloring in spaces to show the data on their *My Graph* graphing sheets (page 138).

5. Students write three statements about their data.

6. You may choose to collect students' recording sheets or have students glue them in their math journals..

Differentiation

- Simplify the process for **below-level learners** by having them ask a *yes* or *no* question, rather than a question with three categories.

- **Above-level learners** may make a double bar graph showing the data for boys and girls.

Survey Says...

Think of a survey question, collect data from your friends, create a bar graph showing the results, and write statements about the data.

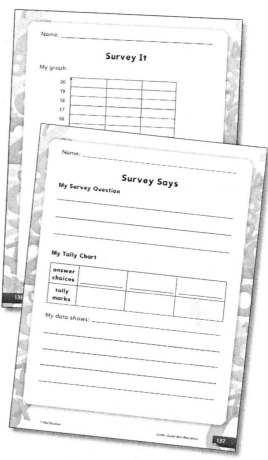

Materials

- *Survey Says* recording sheet
- *My Graph* graphing sheet

Directions

1. Choose a survey question to ask your friends.

2. Write the survey question and three responses on your *Survey Says* recording sheet.

3. Ask your friends to answer the question. Make a tally mark for each response.

4. Color in boxes on your *My Graph* graphing sheet to show the data.

5. Write three statements describing your data.

Talking Points

Vocabulary

- survey
- response
- collect
- category
- data
- tally marks
- bar graph

Talk like a mathematician:

My answer choices are _____, _____ and _____.

More people chose _____ than _____.

Most people chose _____.

Fewest people chose _____.

My graph of the data shows _____.

✂ -

Talking Points

Vocabulary

- survey
- response
- collect
- category
- data
- tally marks
- bar graph

Talk like a mathematician:

My answer choices are _____, _____ and _____.

More people chose _____ than _____.

Most people chose _____.

Fewest people chose _____.

My graph of the data shows _____.

Name: _____

Survey Says

My Survey Question

_____

_____

_____

My Tally Chart

answer choices	_____	_____	_____
tally marks			

My data shows: _____

_____

_____

_____

_____

Name: _____

My Graph

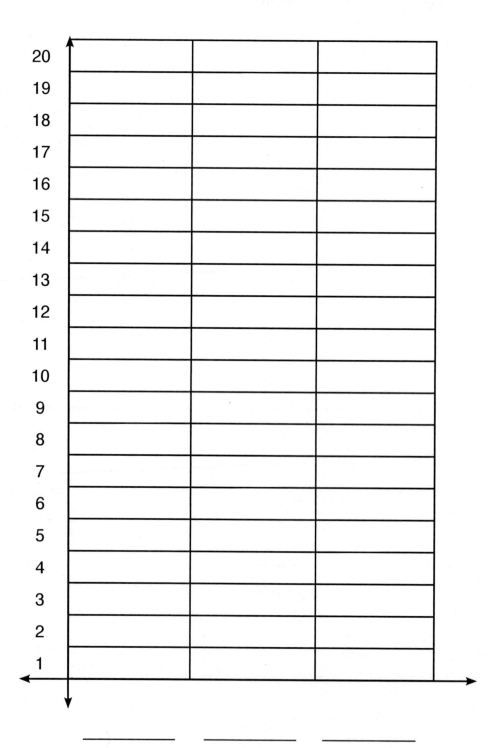

20
19
18
17
16
15
14
13
12
11
10
9
8
7
6
5
4
3
2
1

_____   _____   _____

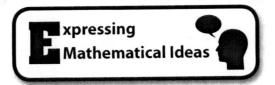

Expressing Mathematical Ideas

All About…

- -

Overview

Students create a poster or digital presentation about a specific number or math topic.

- -

Materials

- chart paper

- crayons, colored pencils, or markers

- devices for taking photographs or videos and for creating a digital presentation (optional)

* The *Talking Points* card and these reproducibles are also provided in the Digital Resources (allabout.pdf).

Objective

Use precise mathematical language, numbers, and/or drawings to represent a mathematical concept.

Procedure

Note: This activity is purposefully unstructured to allow for a great deal of student choice and creativity. You may structure it as an activity to be completed in one class period, or allow students to stretch it into a longer project.

1. Distribute materials to students.

2. One option is for students to choose a number and then represent that number in as many ways as possible. Have students create either posters or digital products, such as digital slideshow presentations. Encourage students to include relevant math vocabulary, pictures representing the number, and real-world connections.

3. Another option is for students to create the same type of product using a math vocabulary term or topic, rather than a number. For example, students might choose addition, subtraction, geometry, or place value.

4. This type of activity allows students to use a wide variety of digital apps that are available to create a product, rather than just using digital apps to practice skills.

Differentiation

This activity adjusts easily for students of all levels. Offering students a choice about the number or topic allows them to choose something within their comfort zone yet still benefit from expressing their ideas using multiple representations.

All About...

Create a product that shows everything you know about a number or a math vocabulary word.

Materials

- chart paper
- crayons, colored pencils, or markers
- devices for taking photos or videos and for creating a digital presentation (optional)

Directions

1. Choose a number, vocabulary word, or math topic.

2. Use words, numbers, and pictures to show everything you can about your number, word, or topic.

3. If you choose a number, think about:
   - different ways to represent the number
   - examples in everyday life
   - personal connections
   - related vocabulary

4. If you choose a vocabulary word or math topic, think about:
   - the meaning of the word
   - pictures or drawings that show the meaning
   - examples and non-examples
   - connections to everyday life
   - related math ideas

Talking Points

Vocabulary	Talk like a mathematician:
• connections • diagram • goal • justify • model • observe • represent	I made a connection between _____ and _____ because _____. I included this representation because _____. This word reminds me of _____. Clearly communicating my ideas is important because _____.

✂ ┈┈┈┈┈┈┈┈┈┈┈┈┈┈┈┈┈┈┈┈┈┈┈┈┈┈┈┈┈┈┈┈┈┈┈┈┈┈

Talking Points

Vocabulary	Talk like a mathematician:
• connections • diagram • goal • justify • model • observe • represent	I made a connection between _____ and _____ because _____. I included this representation because _____. This word reminds me of _____. Clearly communicating my ideas is important because _____.

References Cited

Diller, Debbie. 2011. *Math Work Stations: Independent Learning You Can Count On, K–2*. Portland: Stenhouse Publishers.

Mathnook. 2016. "MathPup Golf." *Cool Math Games for Kids*. Last modified November 29, 2016. www.mathnook.com

Sammons, Laney. 2010. *Guided Math: A Framework for Mathematics Instruction*. Huntington Beach: Shell Education.

———. 2013. *Strategies for Implementing Guided Math*. Huntington Beach: Shell Education.

———. 2014. *Guided Math Conferences*. Huntington Beach: Shell Education.

Digital Resources

Page(s)	Resource	Filename
16–20	*Shake and Spill*	shake.pdf
22–25	*Squeeze Play*	squeeze.pdf
27–30	*Race to the Bottom*	race.pdf
32–39	*Crazy Clock Keep-Away*	crazyclock.pdf
41–42	*Exploring Manipulatives*	manipulatives.pdf
44–46	*Polygon Pictures*	polygon.pdf
48–52	*You Write the Story*	story.pdf
54–59	*What Is the Question?*	question.pdf
61–67	*Representing Numbers*	representing.pdf
69–73	*Missing Number Puzzles*	missing.pdf
75–81	*Piggy Bank Problems*	piggybank.pdf
83–90	*Numberless Word Problems*	numberless.pdf
92–96	*Make 5, Capture 4*	make5.pdf
98–102	*Make 10, Capture 4*	make10.pdf
104–107	*Addition Move One*	moveone.pdf
109–119	*Sum or Difference*	sumordiff.pdf
121–124	*Par for the Course*	par.pdf
126–133	*Math Vocabulary Book*	vocabbook.pdf
135–138	*Survey Says…*	survey.pdf
140–141	*All About…*	allabout.pdf

Notes